# Deep Breath Healing Gardens

## Creating a Personalized Healing Garden For Your Loved One

### By AMA

Copyright © 2024 AMA

## Cover Artwork by Zina Dean-Henderson

All rights reserved. No part of this publication may be reproduced, distributed, or transmitted in any form or by any means without the prior written permission of the publisher, except for brief quotations in reviews.

However, by purchasing this book, you are granted permission to utilize the principles, ideas, questionnaire, and lists contained herein for the purpose of creating personalized healing gardens. Let these concepts flourish and benefit others, spreading like Crazy Little Dandelions!

For permissions inquiries or further information, please contact anne@allenlanddesign.com

**ISBN: 979-8-8693-8074-6**

**"Nature itself is the best physician"**

- Hippocrates

**"And into the forest I go
to lose my mind and find my soul"**

- John Muir

# Table of Contents

Bring Comfort and Inspiration to Your Loved One … 1

History and Benefits of Healing Gardens … 3

Foundation of Personalization – Getting Started … 5

Gathering the Essentials – Functional Garden Elements … 11

Hunting for Treasures – Personalizing the Space … 15

Steps to Bringing the Garden to Life – Tricks of the Trade … 22

Unveiling the Gift and Photos of the Deep Breath Healing Gardens … 25

Seasons and Simplicity – Considerations for Easy Maintenance … 35

Budgeting and Sourcing … 37

A Groovy Hiker's Haven … 40

A Beach Oasis … 42

Placeholder for an Italian Village … 44

Making a Difference – Author Bio and Nonprofit Contact … 46

Questionnaire, Checklists and Note Pages … 50

# Bringing Comfort and Inspiration to Your Loved One

Welcome to the world of personalized healing gardens, where you can transform a simple outdoor spot into a haven of comfort, serenity, and rejuvenation.

Often the news of a loved one being diagnosed with a debilitating disease leaves us feeling sad and helpless and wishing there was something we could do. I know this is how I felt shortly after receiving the news that my good friend Doro was diagnosed with cancer. I was upset for her and her family and wanted to show my love and support, but I really did not know how to do this in a caring yet unobtrusive gesture.

These thoughts were going through my mind while I was relaxing in my little garden she-shed. Additionally, I was aware of my other very conflicting feelings; I was so content sitting in my cozy oasis, surrounded by my favorite stuff—safe in this small, sweet garden sanctuary I had created for myself.

It was then that I knew exactly what I would do: I would make Doro her own she-shed, a recovery zone, a special space, somewhere to relax when she returned home from her upcoming treatments. The day of Doro's first chemo appointment, her daughters and I sprang into action on the back deck. All the furniture and gathered items we had hidden away were all set up in time for her return. What a surprise! Doro loved it.

She called it her good spot.

By following the simple steps in this guide and tapping into the power of nature, you will be able to provide your friend with a healing space that reflects his or her unique personality and journey.

# History and Benefits of Healing Gardens

Healing gardens are not new; they have a rich history that spans cultures and centuries.

In ancient China, traditional healing practices integrated nature as an essential element, emphasizing the balance of energies within the body and the surrounding environment. During the Middle Ages, monasteries in Europe cultivated gardens that served both spiritual and medicinal purposes, and in the early nineteenth century, Florence Nightingale identified the importance of nature and fresh air in hospitals.

Today, Nightingale's advocacy for clean, fresh spaces can be found in large healing gardens at hospitals and health care facilities, where they provide refuge to patients, family and staff.

But your very own sanctuary, filled with garden memories from childhood and favorite colors and scents, with nods to your hobbies and passions, and, most important, a very comfortable lounge chair that you can sink into and take a nap — these are not so common!

# Garden Benefits

**Vitamin D**: Exposure to sunlight in nature can help the body produce vitamin D, which is important for bone health and can have other health benefits.

**Spiritual benefits**: When you are struggling with serious health issues, spending time in nature can provide a sense of spirituality and connectedness to something larger than yourself. This can provide comfort and support during a difficult time and may help with coping and emotional well-being.

**Nature promotes healing**: Spending time in nature has been shown to have a positive effect on the body's ability to heal. Studies have shown that exposure to nature can reduce inflammation, lower blood pressure, boost the immune system, and promote overall healing, which can be particularly important for patients who may be undergoing depleting medical treatments.

# Foundation of Personalization

You like this idea or maybe you love it! But before diving headfirst into creating this personalized haven, you must first ensure that your loved one is interested and will use this space.

I suggest a simple get-together over a cup of tea. During this visit, express to your person how much he or she means to you and convey your heartfelt desire to present him or her with a meaningful gift.

For those of you who are feeling apprehensive about broaching the topic, fearing awkward conversation or inadvertently saying the wrong thing about their illness, take a deep breath and relax. In my experience, most individuals navigating health challenges are fatigued from the constant dialogue surrounding their condition. Shifting the focus to the uplifting notion of flowers, colors, and scents often comes as a tremendous relief. It offers a welcomed respite from the rigors of medical discussions, providing an opportunity for shared joy and anticipation.

## A Friendly Interview

Grab another cup of tea and let's dive in. It's time to get down to business! Welcome to the heart of the garden, where the magic truly happens. Think of this as a friendly interview session, in which we uncover the likes, preferences, passions, and cherished memories that will infuse your garden with personal touches and make it truly unique. As you chat, leave plenty of room for stories to unfold and for those little sparks of smiles and remembrances to light up the conversation. These are the moments that give us invaluable hints about what will truly make the garden space magical.

In the back of this book, you'll find my special questionnaire, meticulously crafted to gather insightful and relevant information. It serves as the blueprint for infusing each garden with its own distinct personality.

## Determine the Space

First, find a safe and easily accessible location for the healing garden. It's important for your loved one to have a private space where he or she can find solace and calm. The average space I create is ten feet by twelve feet. Take into consideration proximity to house—the closer, the better—the availability of shade, views, privacy, distance from noisy neighbors, and level ground. Don't be detoured by ugly or exposed spaces. A colorful outdoor curtain can give the feel of containment and privacy and can block unwanted views.

Some spots are more obvious than others, but having more of the above elements available will make your installation easier.

Every garden is different—just like people.

# Gathering the Essentials

Give yourself some time to sit with your gathered information. This is a special space; don't try to cram it into your to-do list! Wait for it to call you into action, and then work from your heart to make sure this space resonates with the love and friendship you feel for your person.

## Site Information

Once you have determined the space and have a good assessment of the needs, preferences, and limitations of your friend, collecting site information should be next on your list.

I find that taking a lot of pictures and good notes saves me a lot of time and backtracking. I've included a site measurements and logistic checklist in the back of the book.

The top items I make note of are the following:

- Views to block—think privacy!
- The closest hose bib—for simple battery-operated timers and hosing down site before installation
- Whether the area is level for placing furniture or needs some grading
- Measurements of space available for furniture, mobility, and room for a friend to visit (an outdoor rug should cover most of this space)
- Electric outlets available nearby for charging electronics
- Whether there is shade available (and if not, will an umbrella be needed?)
- Location of noisy or nosy neighbors

# Nurturing Necessities

In the creation of a personalized healing garden, certain elements play pivotal roles in enhancing comfort, relaxation, and overall well-being. Each component serves a specific purpose, contributing to the ambiance and functionality of the space.

You will use a large portion of your budget on these items. In the budgeting section, I have some friendly tips for sourcing these materials and ideas to help keep the costs down.

And finally, this is the base for your color scheme. Incorporate the shades or complementary colors that make your loved one happy.

## Chair with ottoman or reclining lounge chair

- ❋ Importance: The place where the relaxation begins, allowing recipients to unwind and immerse themselves into the healing environment.

- ❋ Considerations: Thick cushions in a color that is one of your person's favorites; chair material preference—wood, metal, or rattan.

## Side table

- ❋ Importance: Offers a convenient surface for placing books, beverages, or personal items within reach, enhancing comfort and accessibility.

- ❋ Considerations: Durable material, size and height, shape, electronic charging connection.

## Outdoor rug

- Importance: Defines seating area, adds warmth, and creates a cozy atmosphere while also providing a comfortable surface for bare feet.

- Considerations: Coordination with the color of the chair cushion; a size large enough for all furniture to fit on comfortably.

## Shade umbrella

- Importance: Offers protection from the sun's harsh rays, allowing the recipient to enjoy a shady spot during hot weather.

- Considerations: Size and height, best location for afternoon shade, adjustability.

## Outdoor curtains

- Importance: Easy screening of unwanted views; instills a feeling of privacy and shelter.

- Considerations: Curtain rod brackets attached to stable fence or independently hung using shepherd's hooks, set securely in ground, with sturdy curtains rods in between each hook.

There are many colors and styles of outdoor curtains available online, and tall shepherd's hooks are available at garden centers.

## Comforting blanket

- ❋ Importance: Offers warmth and coziness during cooler weather or early evenings, encouraging extended time in the garden.
- ❋ Considerations: Material preferences; favorite color or complimentary color for coordination.

## Solar-powered twinkle lights

- ❋ Importance: Brings a touch of magic to the garden, creating a soothing and enchanting atmosphere for evening relaxation.
- ❋ Considerations: Recipient's preference for amount of light and placement.

## Favorite mug

- ❋ Importance: Provides a familiar and comforting touch.
- ❋ Considerations: Great mug choices available, possible theme of their hobby; add a box of their favorite tea on the side.

# Hunting for Treasures

In the delightful journey of creating a personalized healing garden, the process of hunting for treasures adds a touch of whimsy and personality, infusing the space with elements that resonate deeply with the recipient's unique spirit and preferences.

Using your person's questionnaire answers; his or her choice of favorite settings; and your conversations of cherished memories, interests, and hobbies, you can embark on this joyful quest.

**This is where your creativity and heart merge to make this a spot that truly nurtures the soul.**

Lila Loves Animé.

Anna's favorite garden memory from childhood is climbing trees.

The color orange makes Charlotte smile.

Incorporate existing items that your person already loves.

## Outdoor Art with Favorite Nature Scene

Infuse the garden with visual delight by incorporating outdoor art featuring the recipient's favorite nature scene, whether it's serene landscapes, vibrant florals, or majestic wildlife.

Seek out local artists, online marketplaces, online banner making companies, or specialty spots offering outdoor-friendly artwork to find the perfect piece that speaks to their heart.

## Tablecloth with Favorite Flowers

Set the stage for al fresco snacking or dining with a tablecloth adorned with the recipient's favorite flowers, bringing bursts of color and cheer to the garden oasis.

Explore home decor stores, artisan markets, or online retailers for tablecloths featuring floral patterns or colors that evoke your person's preferred blooms.

## Weird Garden Gnome or Other Silly or Beautiful Element

I encourage a well-placed hint of whimsy and charm, reflecting your friend's playful spirit, calm presence, or sense of humor.

Embrace creativity and imagination by browsing garden centers, flea markets, or antique shops for unique and unexpected finds that capture his or her personality.

## Lightweight Plant Containers

Add pops of color and texture to the garden with containers filled with your person's favorite flowers, creating vibrant focal points and inviting spots for contemplation.

You'll find these in garden supply stores or online retailers, or you can use DIY options for playful and versatile plant containers that suit your person's taste and style.

## Journal, Notebook, or Small Sketchbook

Encouraging reflection, creativity, and expression by providing a writing or drawing book where the recipient can record thoughts, ideas, and moments of inspiration amid the tranquil surroundings of the garden.

Choose a journal with a design that resonates with his or her aesthetic preferences, whether elegant, whimsical, or nature inspired. Consider adding personalized touches such as initials or a meaningful quote.

## Throw Pillows

Elevate comfort and coziness with throw pillows in vibrant hues and patterns, inviting relaxation and leisurely lounging in the garden oasis.

Search in home decor stores, specialty boutiques, or online retailers for throw pillows that reflect your person's favorite colors, motifs, or themes.

## Nod to Hobbies and Interests

Pay homage to your friend's passions and interests by incorporating elements that speak to his or her hobbies, such as gardening, birdwatching, cooking, or hiking.

Personalize the space with items such as gardening tools, bird feeders, recipe books, or waterproof posters of nature scenes.

## Favorite Memory from Childhood

Weave a thread of nostalgia and warmth by integrating a nod to your person's favorite memory from carefree younger days. You could use a beloved toy, a cherished storybook, or a scent that evokes fond recollections.

Engage in heartfelt conversations and reminiscences during the friendly interview to uncover cherished memories, and incorporate them into the garden design, creating a space imbued with sentimental significance and emotional resonance.

# Bringing the Garden to Life ~ Tricks of the Trade

## Key Elements

In this chapter, we explore simple yet effective tricks of the trade to bring your personalized healing garden to life, ensuring both functionality and restorative benefits. From selecting plants with therapeutic properties to optimizing layout and enduring safety, these practical tips will guide you in creating a nurturing and inviting outdoor sanctuary.

### Creating a Safe and Inviting Pathway

If necessary, create a pathway to guide your friend and visitors safely to the garden, especially if there are uneven surfaces or obstacles.

Ensure pathway materials are slip resistant and well maintained, and consider adding lighting for evening use.

### Optimizing Layout for Comfort and Functionality

Position the chair, table, and other elements in a layout that maximizes comfort, accessibility, and interaction with nature.

Create focal points with plants, art, or other decorative elements to enhance visual interest and create a sense of balance in the garden space.

## Simple Irrigation Solutions

Consider installing a simple drip irrigation system to ensure plants receive consistent moisture without the need for daily watering. You may need to outsource this task, as it is important that it is done correctly. Leaks and surprising sprays of water are not relaxing!

Alternatively, set up a watering can station and schedule so that visitors can participate in nurturing the garden, fostering a sense of connection and engagement with the space.

## Soil Preparation and Drainage Considerations

At your local garden center purchase bags of soil labeled "Container Mix." At the base of each container, start with a layer of large gravel and top with weed cloth. Then add your soil, compacting as you go so plants don't sink after a few waterings as soil compacts itself. Make sure the bottom of the planter has drainage holes.

## Low Maintenance and Therapeutic Plants

Select plants that not only require minimal upkeep but also offer therapeutic benefits, such as aromatic herbs and sensory-rich foliage. Opt for easy-to-grow varieties such as lavender, rosemary, and mint, which not only add beauty to the garden but also provide calming scents and tactile experiences.

If you are a novice gardener, your local nursery would love to help you with the choices. Let them know what you are creating, and let their expertise of plants in your area guide your decision.

If your budget permits, strategically placing a couple of fifteen-gallon container shrubs will add a cozy, nestled-in-the-garden ambiance to the area.

## Day One—Prepare the Canvas

- ❋ Clear everything out of the space and start with a clean palette. Remove any weeds, debris, or cobwebs.
- ❋ If appropriate, level the ground to ensure stability for the lounge chair.
- ❋ Hose everything down to remove dust, dirt, snail trails, and so forth.
- ❋ At the nearest hose bib, set up your timer and drip irrigation line.
- ❋ Assemble the furniture as needed.
- ❋ Note how sunny or shady the area is throughout the day.

## Day Two—Create the Magic

- ❋ Soak in the space. Now that you have a beautifully clean palette, determine the best angles for furniture placement.
- ❋ Roll out the carpet; this really defines the space.
- ❋ Set up the lounge chair and side table, leaving room for maneuvering or pulling up an extra chair for a visitor.
- ❋ Add the planted containers, with saucers to catch water, at edges of carpeted area or, if close, in front of the hose bib to hide the irrigation timer.
- ❋ Place the favorite mug and warm blanket within easy reach.
- ❋ Hang the solar twinkle lights to infuse the space with enchantment.
- ❋ Install the outdoor curtains to offer privacy.
- ❋ Set up the umbrella where it will provide afternoon shade.

# Unveiling the Gift

As we approach the moment of revealing this gift to your loved one, take into consideration his or her personality and aim for a simple yet meaningful way to introduce the garden for the first time. Explaining a little of the process and your reasons for selecting certain items alleviates the pressure of anticipating expected reactions.

It is always fun to see before and after photos, and they help ensure the unveiling is a moment of joy and appreciation for both the giver and the recipient.

Joyce had a small deck that never felt welcoming; she is also a practicing Buddhist.

Featuring a Buddha privacy screen from Home Depot combined with a lovely metal art piece of the Tree of Life, Joyce finally was able to enjoy this Zen Zone alone or with her friends.

Tara just needed a little corner of her garden that wasn't taken over by kids, toys, and sports.

One of her favorite garden memories was the movie FernGully, so I doubled down on ferns. I even found a fern outdoor rug online and made her a lush, toy-free, adults-only zone.

Purple is Susan's favorite color, and she wanted the space to also feel comfortable for her teenage daughter.

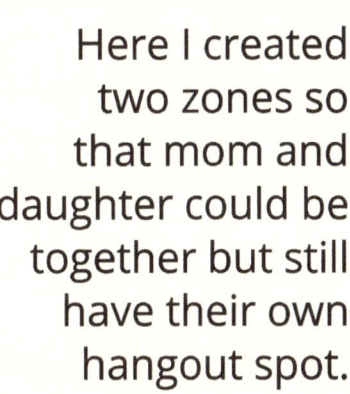

Here I created two zones so that mom and daughter could be together but still have their own hangout spot.

This birdwatching couple with a lovely large garden needed a spot in the shade to relax and appreciate all the work they had done.

To get them into some deep shade, I pruned back an area that was overgrown. Using outdoor curtains gave a sense of enclosure so that their space felt separate from the shrubbery.

Jules had a blank slate to work with. Teal and mustard are her favorite colors.

A nearby hose bib allowed for easy setup of a simple drip irrigation line that wrapped all around the garden space, enabling me to surround the area with low-maintenance plant material.

Jendala lives on a ranch and really needed some privacy from crews getting tools each morning.

The magic of outdoor curtains strikes again!

Since there was nothing to attach curtain brackets to, I used a garden supply center shepherd's hook, generally used for hanging baskets of plants. These hooks held hanging curtain rods instead!

Beautiful metal art work created by
Deep Breath Recipient Jendala - https://jendala.com

# Seasons and Simplicity

Your healing garden is like a living canvas evolving with the seasons. As some items may be weather sensitive, it's crucial to adapt the garden to accommodate different weather conditions while ensuring minimal maintenance and maximum enjoyment.

## Weather-Sensitive Materials

For furniture and decorations, lay a sturdy foundation for year-round durability and aesthetic appeal. By opting for resilient materials, such as treated wood, metal, or weatherproof fabrics, you can minimize the need for frequent upkeep and prolong the life span of your main elements.

## Maintenance

It is important this space is relaxing for recipient.

Let's talk simplicity. Along with installing a battery-operated timer and drip line to automatically water the low-maintenance plants you have chosen, a small handheld electric leaf blower can be an important addition to the garden space. Easily stowed away when not in use, it becomes a discreet yet invaluable asset in keeping the garden pristine and welcoming.

Furthermore, don't hesitate to enlist the helping hands of visitors in maintaining the garden's charm and allure. By empowering guests to lend a hand with light upkeeping tasks, such as sweeping leaves or watering plants, you ensure that the recipient's sole responsibility is to relax and bask in the serenity of his or her personalized sanctuary. You also give friends and family a way of participating in the healing and a tangible way of showing their love and concern.

# Budgeting and Sourcing

In this chapter, we'll explore strategies for budgeting and sourcing materials to create a personalized healing garden that is both cost-effective and tailored to the recipient's needs and preferences. From identifying key investments to leveraging community support, we'll cover all the bases to ensure a successful and fulfilling garden project.

## Budgeting

The most critical and potentially costly element in your healing garden will likely be the lounge chair. Investing in a sturdy, well-made chair with thick, comfortable cushions is essential for providing your friend with a cozy and inviting space to relax and unwind. While this may be a significant upfront expense, it's crucial for ensuring long-term comfort and enjoyment.

Additionally, consider using existing items that the recipient already owns or friends may be willing to donate. Repurposing furniture or decor items not only adds sentimental value but also helps keep costs down. Signing up as a group to purchase items on the list can also spread out the financial burden and make the project more manageable for everyone involved.

Based on my experience, the average cost of installing one of these helpful healing havens typically ranges between $800 and $1,500. This budget encompasses essential elements such as furniture, decor, plants, and materials, allowing for a well-rounded and functional garden space.

## Sourcing

When you are sourcing materials for your garden project, be sure to explore a variety of options to find the best deals and highest quality items. Here are some recommended sourcing spots to consider:

**Local Retailers:** Whenever possible, prioritize shopping at your local nursery and hardware store. Not only does this support small businesses in your community, but the staff can also provide valuable advice and assistance with irrigation questions and plant selection for your area.

**Consignment Stores and Antique Shops:** Explore these spaces for unique and budget-friendly decor items, such as outdoor art, vintage planters, and quirky or beautiful garden treasures.

**Large Home Improvement Stores (Home Depot, Lowe's, T.J. Max, Target):** These are excellent resources for essential garden supplies, including furniture, planters, and tools.

**Online Retailers (Wayfair, Overstock, Amazon):** These offer a wide selection of decor and accessories at competitive prices. This option also allows you to create a simple digital vision board with all the elements to see how they look together.

## Community Support - Like a meal train but more fun!

Finally, don't hesitate to reach out to friends, family, and community members for support in building your healing garden. Many people will be eager to contribute so that they can feel like they are making a meaningful difference in their loved one's journey.

Together you can create a beautiful and nurturing space that brings comfort and joy to your friend's life.

In the back of book, I have created a sign-up sheet that you can use to enlist the help and support of your community. It's similar to a meal train but can be much more fun for some of us!

## Spring Street Botanicals ~

Offering herbal remedies to enhance strengths and balance challenges.

Selected products generously donated to recipients of Deep Breath Healing Gardens non-profit.

https://www.springstreetbotanicals.com/about

# A Groovy Hikers' Haven

Discover the story of Amy, a woman who adores hiking and the color orange. We determined that a protected corner of her side yard was the spot for her space and decided to tie in the existing barbecue area for family get-togethers.

Using outdoor curtains attached to the back fence posts, we screened the neighbor's house, giving Amy a sense of privacy. Adding a large outdoor rug helped ground the space, level out the dirt, and stabilize from existing gopher holes. I found an online banner site, downloaded a picture of a mountain lake, and then turned it into a waterproof piece of art. Finally, incorporating some of Amy's original mosaic artwork allowed this renovated space to become her haven for relaxation and rejuvenation.

# A Beach Oasis

Marion loves going to the beach, gardening, and reading. She wanted a private space to sit with friends for tea.

For her garden we transformed a small corner of her outdoor space into a tranquil beach oasis. We collected driftwood, shells, and mermaid decor to bring the soothing vibes of the sea to her garden.

As her garden was more for visiting than lounging, I chose these awesome mermaid chairs, found at T.J. Maxx. They are more upright than the usual choice, but remember—every garden is different!

# Placeholder for an Italian Village

Meet Judy, a woman who lives in a mobile home park, loves to travel, and is always surrounded by family and friends. Due to her cancer diagnosis, Judy had to cancel her much-anticipated trip to Italy.

So while Judy was away for the weekend, I was able to transform a corner spot of her outdoor space into a cozy little terrazza! I filled her large terracotta plant containers with lovely dark-purple smoke bushes and red geraniums and softened the paneling between properties with café-like striped outdoor curtains. I found the perfect wall hanging of an Italian cobblestone street that I attached to her fence. An outdoor chair with footstool set the stage for future trip planning.

# Making a Difference ~ Planting Seeds of Hope

Anne-Marie Allen, a glorious garden designer with more than three decades of expertise in crafting exquisite landscapes, has established herself as a respected figure in Sonoma County, California. Her career and her company, Allen Land Design, trajectory is marked by the creation and installation of award-winning high-end residential and commercial gardens, interesting plant combinations, and meticulous attention to detail.

Drawing on her extensive experience, knowledge, and expertise, Anne-Marie approaches each project with a profound sense of passion and dedication. With a unique blend of artistry and horticultural expertise, she transforms small spaces into personalized havens of tranquility and healing.

In this book, she generously shares her wealth of knowledge and tricks of the trade, empowering readers to create their own personalized healing spaces for loved ones. With clarity and insight, Anne-Marie demystifies the process, providing practical guidance and inspiration for novice gardeners and seasoned enthusiasts alike.

In addition to her commercial endeavors, Anne-Marie is deeply committed to philanthropic efforts through her nonprofit organization, Deep Breath Healing Gardens. She seeks to inspire fellow gardeners and landscape businesses to follow suit in offering these rejuvenating spaces as a heartfelt gesture of compassion and goodwill to their community and clients.

Join her and donate at www.deepbreathgardens.com.

Anne-Marie's magical touch infuses every garden she creates with a sprinkle of love; she crafts each element to evoke a sense of serenity and well-being.

Company Motto!

# Deep Breath Healing Gardens

When you are all finished with your garden, please email me before-and-after pictures. If you include your address, I will send you one of my motto stickers!

anne@allenlanddesign.com

# Questionnaire, Checklists, Sign-Up Sheets and Note Pages

Donations to Deep Breath Gardens non-profit appreciated for sharing copies of these materials: www.deepbreathgardens.com.

# Questionnaire
# A Few Friendly Questions

❈ What colors do you like to see? Be specific (e.g., baby blue, dark purple, lemon yellow).

❈ When I say to you, "Picture yourself in a beautiful garden," what are a few words that come to mind?

❈ What are your favorite smells?

❈ What are your hobbies, passions, and interests?

❈ For an outdoor rug, do you want a pattern or solid? Jazz it up or keep it mellow?

❈ Do you have a green thumb or want clean hands?

❈ Do you have any garden memories of childhood?

❈ Do you like dappled sun or deep shade?

❈ Do you have a favorite tea?

❈ Do you want a chair with an ottoman or a reclining lounge chair?

❈ Are there any colors you do not like?

❈ Are there any pieces of garden art or furniture that you would like me to incorporate into this healing garden?

# In which of these settings would you feel most relaxed?

_____ Jungle Love - tropical, lush, green

_____ Classy but Sassy - understated colors with splashes of your favorite color

_____ Zen Zone - Clean lines, modern plants, a simple space, monochromatic

_____ Breath of fresh - Colorful, flowery, cheerful

# Essentials Checklist

_____A comfortable lounge chair, with thick cushions, for relaxation

_____Throw pillows in one of the recipient's favorite colors

_____A small side table to hold personal items and necessities

_____An outdoor rug to define the space and add coziness. This item should incorporate the color of chair cushion and be twice the size of the lounge chair

_____A favorite mug for warm beverages

_____A soft and comforting blanket—keep with the favorite color theme or a complementary color

_____Solar-powered twinkle lights to bring a touch of magic

_____Outdoor curtains or an umbrella for shade

# Site Measurements and Logistics

_____Locate hose bib.

_____Is good shade available?

_____Is an umbrella needed?

_____What size outdoor rug will fit?
Make sure it's big enough for all furniture to fit comfortably.

_____Is there anything unsightly that will need screening or blocking for privacy?

_____Basic tools needed for installation
broom, rake, blower, flat shovel for leveling, hand trowel for planting in containers, planting soil, drain rock, weed cloth, irrigation materials, screw gun for hanging treasures, hose with nozzle

_____What existing garden items and furniture can be incorporated into healing garden? (Ask first.)

_____Look for an electrical outlet for electronic charging.

# Garden Creation Sample Supply & Sign-Up Sheet

Thank you for your willingness to contribute to the creation of a personalized healing garden for our loved one, _____. Your support is invaluable in bringing this special sanctuary to life. Please sign up below for any items you would like to provide or help procure, as well as any other contributions you are able to offer. If you have questions regarding budget, style or where to find items, please call me.

Your Name_____ Your Phone Number_____

## Item Contributions:

Comfortable Lounge Chair or Adjustable Chair with footstool or ottoman

    Provided by:_____

Side Table

    Provided by:_____

Outdoor Rug

    Provided by:_____

Shade Umbrella

    Provided by:_____

Beautiful Mug with Box of Favorite Tea

    Provided by:_____

Warm Blanket

    Provided by:_____

Solar-Powered Twinkle Lights

    Provided by:_____

Table Covering with Favorite Flowers or Colors

    Provided by:_____

Outdoor Art with Favorite Nature Scene

    Provided by:_____

Quirky Garden Gnome or Other Decorative Element

    Provided by:_____

Fun Lightweight Plant Containers

    Provided by:_____

Plants

    Provided by:_____

Soil, Drain Rock, Weed Cloth

    Provided by:_____

Journal, Notebook, or Sketchbook

    Provided by:_____

Throw Pillows

    Provided by:_____

Small Handheld Electric Blower

    Provided by:_____

# Notes, Ideas, and Reminders

# Sketches, Doodles, and Diagrams

www.ingramcontent.com/pod-product-compliance
Lightning Source LLC
LaVergne TN
LVHW070533070526
838199LV00075B/6773